SACRED TEXTS

The Qur'an
and Islam

Anita Ganeri

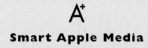

Smart Apple Media

Evans Brothers Limited
2A Portman Mansions
Chiltern St.
London W1U 6NR

First published 2003
Text copyright © Anita Ganeri 2003
© in the illustrations Evans Brothers Ltd 2003

Printed in Hong Kong by Wing King Tong Co. Ltd

Editors: Nicola Barber, Louise John
Designer: Simon Borrough
Illustrations: Tracy Fennell, Allied Artists
Production: Jenny Mulvanny
Consultant: Usamah K Ward, The Muslim
Educational Trust

Picture acknowledgements:
theartarchive: p6 (Dagli Orti)
Circa Photo Library: p10, p15 top (William Holtby),
p21 bottom (William Holtby), p22 (John Smith), p23
(William Holtby), p25 bottom
Hutchison Library: p17
Peter Sanders: p7, p8, p9, p11, p12, p13, p15 bottom,
p16, p18, p19, p21 top, p25 top, p26, p27

Published in the United States by
Smart Apple Media, 1980 Lookout Drive
North Mankato, Minnesota 56003

Library of Congress Cataloging-in-Publication Data

Ganeri, Anita.
The Qur'an and Islam / by Anita Ganeri ;
illustrated by Tracy Fennell.
p. cm. — (Sacred texts)
Includes index.
Summary: Explains the history and practices of the
religion of Islam, especially as revealed through its
sacred book, the Koran.
Contents: Origins — Structure and contents —
Message and teachings — Daily life and worship —
Study and reading.
ISBN 1-58340-241-1
1. Islam—Doctrines—Juvenile literature. 2. Koran—
Doctrines—Juvenile literature. [1. Islam—
Doctrines. 2. Koran.] I. Fennell, Tracy, ill. II. Title.
III. Sacred texts (Mankato, Minn.)

BP165.5.G36 2003
297.2—dc21   2002042797

First Edition
9 8 7 6 5 4 3 2 1

The quotations in this book come from a translation of the Qur'an published by Saheeh International, Abul-Qasim Publishing House, 1997.

In this book, dates are written using B.C.E., which means "before the common era," and C.E., which means "of the common era." These abbreviations replace B.C. ("before Christ") and A.D. (*anno domini*, "in the year of the Lord"), which are based on the Christian calendar.

In each of the world's six main religions—Buddhism, Christianity, Hinduism, Islam, Judaism, and Sikhism—sacred texts play an important part. They teach people how to practice their faith and guide them through their lives. Wherever these books are read or studied, they are treated with great care and respect because they are so precious.

Contents

Introduction

The Holy Qur'an

The Holy Qur'an is the sacred book of the Muslims, who follow the religion of Islam. The word "Islam" means "submission" in the Arabic language. Muslims believe in one God, whom they call Allah. They submit to (obey) Allah's will and try to live in a way that is pleasing to Him. They believe that Allah revealed His wishes for the world to a man called the Prophet Muhammad ﷺ (Muslims often write the Arabic symbol ﷺ after the names of the prophets. It means "peace and blessings upon him.") Muhammad ﷺ was the last and greatest in a line of prophets chosen by Allah to teach people how to live. The messages sent from Allah to the Prophet Muhammad ﷺ were later collected together to make the Qur'an.

A picture of Makkah in the 19th century. The Prophet Muhammad ﷺ was born here in about 570 C.E.

How Islam began

Islam began about 1,400 years ago in the city of Makkah, in the country now called Saudi Arabia. This is where Muhammad ﷺ was born in 570 C.E. Muhammad's ﷺ father died before he was born, and his mother died when he was six. Muhammad ﷺ was brought up first by his grandfather, then by his uncle. At that time, Makkah was an important center of trade, and Muhammad ﷺ worked as a merchant. When he was 25 years old, he married a wealthy widow, named Khadijah.

The holy book

Muslims believe that the Qur'an is the direct word of Allah, as revealed to the Prophet Muhammad ﷺ through the angel Jibril (Gabriel). They say that the Qur'an has always existed in heaven, written in Arabic on a tablet of stone. Muslims respect and honor the Qur'an, and use it as a guide for their lives. The Qur'an teaches them how to worship, how to treat other people, and how to live good lives.

Islam today

Today, there are about one billion Muslims living all over the world. Islam is the official religion of countries such as Pakistan, Bangladesh, and Iran. Most countries in the Middle East are Muslim. The worldwide family of Muslims is called the Ummah. Wherever they have settled and whatever language they speak, all Muslims have a duty to read and understand the Qur'an.

A Muslim girl reading the Holy Qur'an. For Muslims, the Qur'an is a very special book because it is believed to be the direct word of Allah (God).

"And We have sent down to you the Book as clarification for all things and as guidance and mercy and good tidings for Muslims."

(Surah 16: 89)

Origins

The Qur'an is revealed

In Muhammad's ﷺ time, the people of Makkah worshipped many different gods at a sacred building called the Ka'bah. Many people grew rich from trade, but they were also cruel and corrupt. These things upset Muhammad ﷺ, who was known for his kindness and honesty. He began to spend more time by himself, thinking and praying. One night, in 610 C.E., when Muhammad ﷺ was 40 years old, he had an experience that changed his life.

The cave of Hira, on Mount Nur, near Makkah. This is where Muhammad ﷺ received the first words of the Qur'an.

An angel appears

Muhammad ﷺ was meditating in a cave called Hira, on Mount Nur (Mountain of Light), near Makkah, when an angel, Jibril, appeared before him and showed him a cloth covered in writing. The angel ordered Muhammad ﷺ to recite the words on the cloth, but Muhammad ﷺ could not read or write. Again and again, the angel commanded him. Suddenly, Muhammad ﷺ knew what the words said and started to recite them. The words began:

"Recite in the name of your Lord who created—Created man from a clinging substance. Recite, and your Lord is the most Generous—Who taught by the pen—Taught man that which he knew not." (SURAH 96: 1-5)

Further revelations

The words of Surah 96 were the first revelation from the Qur'an. (A revelation is a message sent by Allah to human beings.) The revelation went on to tell Muhammad ﷺ that he must stop the people of Makkah from leading selfish lives and bring them closer to Allah.

Muslim pilgrims walk around the sacred Ka'bah building in Makkah.

Over the next 23 years, Muhammad ﷺ received many more revelations. He did not always see the angel Jibril. Sometimes he heard a voice speaking to him, or a sound like a clanging bell. Some revelations came when he was praying. Others happened when he was talking to people or going about his everyday life. Muhammad ﷺ was deeply affected by the revelations. He said that he felt like his soul was being snatched away.

Muslims believe that angels are heavenly beings, created by Allah out of light. They are Allah's servants and can take any form they like to carry out the commands of Allah. One of the most important angels is Jibril, who brought Allah's message to the prophets. Every person has two guardian angels who record their good and bad deeds in a book.

"This is a Book which We have revealed to you, O Muhammad ﷺ, that you might bring mankind out of darknesses into the light by permission of their Lord—to the path of the Exalted in Might, the Praiseworthy—Allah, to whom belongs whatever is in the heavens and whatever is on the earth." (SURAH 14: 1-2)

The beginnings of Islam

After the first revelation, Muhammad ﷺ went home and told his family what had happened. His wife, Khadijah, believed that he had been called to be Allah's prophet and became his first follower. Muhammad ﷺ started to teach people about how Allah wanted them to live. Many people in Makkah listened to Muhammad ﷺ and accepted Islam. But some did not like his teachings and accused him of being a troublemaker. Nonbelievers persecuted the early Muslims and made their lives very difficult.

The Night Journey

Ten years after the first revelation, Muhammad's ﷺ wife and uncle died. They had been Muhammad's ﷺ closest supporters. Then an amazing thing happened, which strengthened Muhammad's ﷺ faith. One night, the angel Jibril woke Muhammad ﷺ and took him on a journey to Jerusalem. This is known as the Night Journey. Jibril took Muhammad ﷺ up through the seven levels of heaven. There, Allah gave Muhammad ﷺ instructions that Muslims must pray five times every day.

The revelations that Muhammad ﷺ received were later written down as the Holy Qur'an.

"Say, if the sea were ink for writing the words of my Lord, the sea would be exhausted before the words of my Lord were exhausted, even if We brought the like of it as a supplement." (SURAH 18: 109)

The flight to Madinah

In Makkah, the persecution of the Muslims continued for many years. In 622 C.E., Muhammad ﷺ and his followers were forced to flee to the city of Madinah, where they were warmly welcomed. This journey became known as the Hijrah, or migration, and marks the beginning of the Muslim calendar. It was in Madinah that Muhammad ﷺ and his followers built the first mosque (see page 22).

The Qur'an tells of many earlier prophets chosen by Allah to receive His message. The most famous include Adam ﷺ, Ibrahim ﷺ (Abraham), Musa ﷺ (Moses), and Isa ﷺ (Jesus), who are also important in Judaism and Christianity. Muhammad ﷺ was the last and greatest of these prophets.

Death of the Prophet

Muhammad ﷺ returned to Makkah in 630 C.E., at the head of a huge army. But instead of fighting, he entered the city in peace. He destroyed the images in the Ka'bah and called on the people of Makkah to worship Allah. Then he returned to Madinah. Two years later, Muhammad ﷺ made the Hajj pilgrimage to the Ka'bah, and went to Mount Arafat to preach his final sermon. When he finished, he received his last revelation:

"This day I have perfected for you your religion and completed My favor upon you and have approved for you Islam as religion." (SURAH 5: 3)

Shortly afterwards, Muhammad ﷺ returned to Madinah, where he died.

The Mosque of the Prophet in Madinah. It was built on the site of Muhammad's ﷺ first mosque.

Structure and Contents

Collecting the Qur'an

Muhammad ﷺ could not read or write. Each time he received a revelation, he memorized the words. Then he recited them to his companions, who also learned them by heart. Muhammad's ﷺ companions then wrote the verses down on pieces of bone, stones, hide, and palm leaves, or any paper-like material they could find. These pages were kept in Muhammad's ﷺ house.

Copying the Qur'an

After the death of Muhammad ﷺ, his closest friend, Abu Bakr, wanted to put the revelations together in one book. A man named Zaid Ibn Thabit collected all the pages of verses together and wrote them down in one place, exactly as Muhammad ﷺ had recited them. He did not change them in any way. This became the standard version of the Qur'an, and all other copies were checked against it. The text of the Qur'an used today is a copy

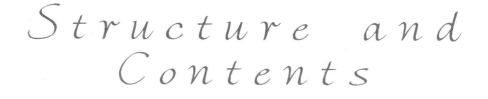

A beautifully decorated, handwritten copy of the Qur'an. It was made during the 18th century.

of Zaid Ibn Thabit's version. Early copies of the Qur'an had to be written out by hand. This took several weeks to complete. Today, modern printing methods mean that thousands of copies can be printed by machine.

"This is the Book about which there is no doubt, a guidance for those conscious of Allah–Who believe in the unseen, establish prayer, and spend out of what We have provided for them. And who believe in what has been revealed to you, O Muhammad ﷺ, and what was revealed before you, and of the Hereafter they are certain in faith." (SURAH 2: 2-4)

Each of the chapters of the Qur'an (except chapter nine) begins with the words: "In the name of Allah, the compassionate, the merciful." These words are known as the Bismillah. In daily life, Muslims say them before they eat a meal or perform a task, to ask for Allah's blessing. It is said that the Bismillah was written on Jibril's wing.

Written in Arabic

The Qur'an is written in Arabic, the language of Muhammad ﷺ and his people. Because Muslims believe that the Qur'an contains the exact words of Allah, it cannot be altered or changed. All devout Muslims try to learn Arabic so they can read the Qur'an, even if it is not their own language. Translations of the Qur'an into other languages are allowed, to help non-Arabic speakers, but they are not thought to have the same authority as the original Arabic version.

Learning by heart

Some of Muhammad's ﷺ companions learned the verses of the Qur'an by heart so that they could recite them to others. Many Muslims still try to do this today as a way of praising Allah. People who know the whole Qur'an by heart are allowed to call themselves huffaz (singular: hafiz). They are highly regarded and respected.

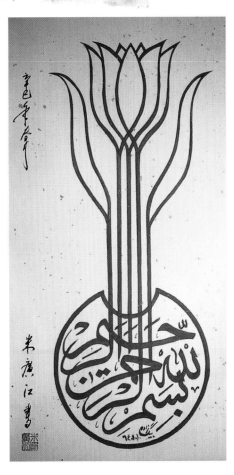

The Bismillah, written in decorative handwriting so that it forms a picture.

A unique book

Muslims believe that the Qur'an is a unique book, with its own style and message. They believe that it is different from other sacred texts because it was composed by Allah, not by human authors. It is also the only holy book to have survived exactly as it was revealed. The Qur'an is not a storybook, with a beginning, a middle, and an end. Instead, it jumps from subject to subject, giving advice and guidance.

Chapters and verses

The Qur'an is divided into 114 chapters, or surahs. They are made up of 6,616 verses called ayats (singular: ayah). The surahs are of different lengths. The shortest is only three verses long; others cover several pages. The chapters always appear in the same order, but this is not the order in which they were revealed to Muhammad ﷺ. The first words to be revealed to Muhammad ﷺ were those of Surah 96: 1-5. The order of the Qur'an was revealed to Muhammad ﷺ later on, and he learned it by heart and recited it to the angel Jibril several times before he died.

Each surah of the Qur'an is named after an unusual word or event that appears in it. Some surahs have strange names, for example, the Cow, the Spider, and the Elephant. The Elephant (Surah 105) is actually about an attack on Makkah by the Governor of Yemen in the year that Muhammad ﷺ was born.

"Say, if mankind and the jinn gathered in order to produce the like of this Qur'an, they could not produce the like of it, even if they were to each other assistants." (SURAH 17: 88) NOTE: A jinn is a good or evil spirit.

Makkah and Madinah

The surahs can be divided into groups—those revealed to Muhammad ﷺ in Makkah, and those revealed in Madinah after the Hijrah. The Makkan surahs are shorter and set out the basic beliefs of Islam. They talk about Allah, creation, and life after death. The Madinan surahs are longer. They cover all aspects of how people should live.

Beautiful writing

Muslims believe that it is wrong to illustrate copies of the Qur'an with pictures of people. This is because people are created by Allah, not by human artists. Instead, Muslims turn the writing itself into a work of art, worthy of Allah's words. This ornamental style of writing is called calligraphy. Calligraphers are highly respected because their writing carries Allah's message. Calligraphy is also used to decorate buildings, tiles, vases, and prayer mats.

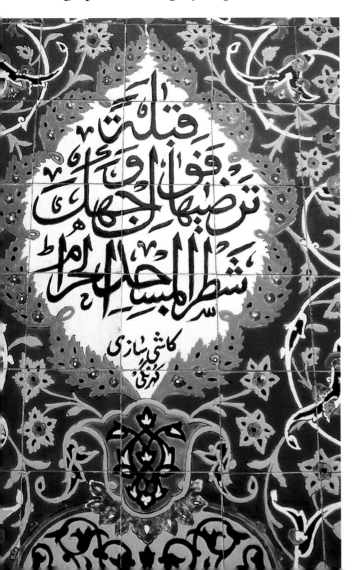

A calligrapher at work. Calligraphers are very skilled and highly respected for their work.

Tiles decorated with a verse from the Qur'an: "A Qiblah (direction of prayer) with which you will be pleased. So turn your face towards al Masjid al Harám (The Sacred Mosque in Makkah)."

Message and Teachings

What the Qur'an teaches

The Qur'an contains the main teachings of Islam. For Muslims, it is the greatest book of guidance from Allah and the basis for their beliefs. Muslims are expected to try their best to understand the Qur'an and to follow its teachings, which cover all aspects of this life and life after death. Many of the verses of the Qur'an were revealed to Muhammad ﷺ when he needed guidance on a particular matter. Muslims believe that when they read or hear the Qur'an, Allah Himself speaks directly to them, offering them support and help.

A Muslim woman praying, using her prayer beads. For each of the beads, she says one of the 99 names of Allah.

About Allah

Muslims believe that Allah is the one and only God. The Qur'an says that Allah sees and knows everything. He has no form nor body, is neither male nor female, and has no beginning nor end. Allah created the world and everything in it, but no one created Allah. Allah is close to everyone who believes in Him. The Qur'an gives 99 beautiful names for Allah. Each name represents one of Allah's qualities, such as compassion or mercy.

Types of beings

The Qur'an tells Muslims how Allah created the world and everything in it. From His throne, He looks after the world and controls what happens in it. Allah created human beings. He also created other types of beings, called angels (see page 9) and jinns. Jinns can be good or evil spirits. Their chief is Shaytan, or the Devil, who tries to lead people away from Allah.

"He is Allah, other than whom there is no deity, Knower of the unseen and the witnessed. He is the Entirely Merciful, the Especially Merciful."

(SURAH 59: 22)

The Day of Judgement

Many teachings about life after death are found in the Qur'an. Muslims believe that on the Last Day, or Day of Judgement, Allah will bring the dead back to life. Each person's book of deeds (see page 9) will be opened, and Allah will judge him or her. If the good deeds outweigh the bad, an angel will lead that person to Paradise. If the bad deeds are heavier, that person will plummet down to Hell. But Allah is a merciful judge. If a person is truly sorry, the bad deeds will be wiped out.

The Qur'an describes Paradise as a beautiful garden, filled with sweet-smelling flowers, shady trees, bird song, and gushing fountains. It is a place of perfect peace and happiness. Muslim rulers often planted exquisite gardens around their palaces. These gardens were designed according to the descriptions of Paradise found in the Qur'an.

The garden at the Alhambra palace in Granada, Spain, which was built in the 13th and 14th centuries.

The Five Pillars of Islam

Muslims show their devotion to Allah by following five practices or duties. These are called the Five Pillars of Islam. Just as real pillars support, or hold up, a building, these practices support Islam. Each of the Five Pillars is mentioned throughout the Qur'an. In his last sermon, Muhammad ﷺ urged Muslims to follow these duties as a way of summing up the basic teachings of their religion.

The first pillar

The first pillar is Shahadah, the declaration of faith. It says: "I bear witness that there is no God except Allah; Muhammad ﷺ is the messenger of Allah." This is the first prayer every Muslim learns. But just saying the words is not enough. Muslims must believe them with all their hearts.

The second pillar

The second pillar is Salah, or prayer. During Muhammad's ﷺ Night Journey (see page 10), Allah told Muhammad ﷺ that Muslims must pray five times a day. The Qur'an says that they must also face the Ka'bah in Makkah. Prayers are said in Arabic and follow a set order of words and actions, taught by Muhammad ﷺ.

Muslims praying. The four main prayer positions are standing, bowing, kneeling, and prostration (lying face down).

"So exalted is Allah when you reach the evening and when you reach the morning. And to Him is due all praise throughout the heavens and the earth. And exalted is He at night and when you are at noon." (SURAH 30: 17–18)

"And spend in the way of Allah and do not throw yourselves with your own hands into destruction by refraining. And do good; indeed, Allah loves the doers of good."

(Surah 2: 195)

Muslim pilgrims walking around the Ka'bah. The embroidered calligraphy on the black cloth covering the Ka'bah is of words from the Qur'an.

The third pillar

The third pillar is Zakah, which means giving a fixed amount of money, jewelry, or goods away. It must be paid every year by those Muslims who can afford it. It must be given only to certain deserving causes, such as the poor and needy, or orphans, as mentioned in the Qur'an.

The fourth pillar

The fourth pillar is Sawm, or fasting during the holy month of Ramadan. This is a very special time for Muslims because it was during Ramadan that Allah sent the first revelations of the Qur'an. Muslims do not eat or drink between daybreak and sunset. By fasting, people learn self-discipline and keep away from selfishness and greed.

The fifth pillar

The fifth pillar is the Hajj, or pilgrimage to Makkah. All Muslims hope to make the Hajj at least once in their lives, if they can afford it, and if they are fit enough to go. At the start of the Hajj, pilgrims walk seven times around the sacred Ka'bah, the House of Allah, which is the holiest building in Islam. During the Hajj, Muslims feel that they are in the presence of Allah, to whom they belong.

19

Daily Life and Worship

The way of the Prophet

Muslims live their lives according to the teachings of the Qur'an and the example set by the Prophet Muhammad ﷺ. The Sunnah is based on what Muhammad ﷺ did and said in his daily life. It is not a book; it is a code of behavior. If Muslims have a problem and cannot find an answer in the Qur'an, they turn to the Sunnah to find out what Muhammad ﷺ might have done in a similar situation. Muslims do not worship Muhammad ﷺ as a god. They love and honor him as their guide and teacher.

The hadith

Some years after Muhammad's ﷺ death, his sayings and accounts of his actions were collected together. They became known as the hadith. The collectors of the hadith travelled far and wide, talking to descendants of people who had known Muhammad ﷺ. Scholars had very strict rules for deciding if a hadith was genuine or not. The two most reliable hadith collections are by Imam al-Bukhari and Imam Muslim. They were collected in the ninth century C.E.

Sometimes new laws are needed to deal with modern developments or events, such as photography or going to the movies. Muslim scholars debate and discuss the issue and try to find an answer, based on their knowledge of the Qur'an and the Sunnah. This might mean comparing a modern issue to something similar in the Qur'an or the Sunnah, and finding a suitable ruling.

"Behold, I have left among you two things. You will never go astray so long as you hold fast to them—the Book of Allah and my Sunnah." (THE HADITH)

Shari'ah law

Together, the Qur'an and the Sunnah form the guidance for Muslims' lives. From them, early Muslim scholars compiled a code of conduct, called the Shari'ah, or path. The Shari'ah gives all the basic rules about how people should live and act, in worshipping Allah, in family matters, and in their dealings with other people and the world. Sometimes the Shari'ah is known as Islamic law.

Giving a fixed amount of money each year to charity is compulsory for Muslims.

Five categories of behavior

To make the Shari'ah easier for ordinary Muslims to follow, there are five categories of behavior. They are:

- Fard—things that are compulsory and must be done, such as keeping the Five Pillars of Islam (see pages 18-19).
- Mustahab—things that are recommended but not compulsory, such as praying more than five times a day.

- Mubah—things that are neither liked nor disliked, but which people must decide for themselves.
- Makruh—things that are disliked but not forbidden, such as getting divorced or wasting time.
- Haram—things that are forbidden, such as smoking and drinking alcohol.

Muslims use the teachings of the Qur'an and the Sunnah to guide them through their lives.

The Qur'an in daily life

The Qur'an is an essential part of a Muslim's everyday life, both at home and in the mosque. It is read and recited during daily prayers, and at times of need, such as when someone is ill or unhappy. Muslims believe that whatever problem they have, they can look in the Qur'an and find the answer. But the Qur'an must be read with faith, otherwise the reader will not benefit from its guidance and wisdom.

Friday prayers

A mosque is a place where Muslims go to worship. Some go to the mosque every day. But all Muslims try to attend the mosque on Fridays for midday prayers, as requested in the Qur'an. Prayers begin with the opening chapter of the Qur'an:

"In the name of Allah, the Entirely Merciful, the Especially Merciful.
All praise is due to Allah, Lord of the Worlds—
The Entirely Merciful, the Especially Merciful.
Sovereign of the Day of Judgement.
It is You we worship and You we ask for help.
Guide us to the straight path—
The path of those upon whom You have bestowed favor, not of those who have evoked Your anger or of those who are astray." (SURAH 1)

In the mosque, the imam leads the prayers and gives a talk, or sermon, at Friday midday prayers.

22

Family life

The Qur'an gives teachings on all aspects of family life, including marriage, divorce, and children. It is the duty of parents to bring up their children to follow Islam. Good manners and education are important, too. Children also have duties to their parents. They must treat their parents with love and respect, and care for them in their old age.

Rules about food

The Qur'an sets out many rules about food and drink. Food which Muslims are allowed to eat is called halal. Forbidden food is called haram. All vegetables, fruits, grains, and fish are halal. Meat is halal if it is killed in a particular way and dedicated to Allah. But pork and any pork products are always haram. Many Muslims buy their food from special halal shops.

"O you who have believed, when the adhan* is called for the prayer on Friday, then proceed to the remembrance of Allah and leave trade. That is better for you, if you only knew. And when the prayer has been concluded, disperse within the land and seek from the bounty of Allah, and remember Allah often that you may succeed." (SURAH 62: 9–10)

*The adhan is the call to prayer from the mosque.

The Qur'an tells people to dress modestly. Many Muslim women wear long clothing and veils over their heads, to cover as much of their bodies (and sometimes their faces) as possible. Muslim men often wear long tunics and baggy trousers. Men and boys should not wear silk or gold jewelry.

Women at prayer. These women are wearing traditional clothing.

Fasting and feasting

During the year, the Qur'an is recited on special occasions, such as festivals. The two most important festivals in the Muslim year are Id-ul-Fitr and Id-ul-Adha. These are times of celebration and joy, as Allah commanded in the Qur'an, as well as times for all Muslims to come together to praise and thank Allah. Verses from the Qur'an are also recited at Muslim weddings and funerals.

The Night of Power

The ninth month of the Muslim year is called Ramadan. This is a particularly holy time because it was during this time that the Qur'an was first revealed to Muhammad ﷺ. The night on which Muhammad ﷺ received the first revelation (see page 8) is called Laylat-ul-Qadr, or the Night of Power. Many Muslims spend the whole night at the mosque, praying and reading the Qur'an. By doing this, they believe that they will be granted the same number of blessings as if they had prayed for a thousand months.

"Indeed, We sent the Qur'an down during the Night of Power.
And what can make you know what is the Night of Power?
The Night of Power is better than a thousand months.
The angels and the Spirit (Jibril) descend therein by permission of their Lord forever matter.
Peace it is until the emergence of dawn." (SURAH 97: 1–5)

During Ramadan, Muslims break their fast with dates and water, following the example of the Prophet Muhammad ﷺ.

Id-ul-Fitr

During Ramadan, Muslims fast from daybreak to sunset every day (see page 19). They celebrate the end of the fast with the festival of Id-ul-Fitr, when Muslims visit the mosque to pray. They thank Allah for sending the Qur'an and giving them the strength to be able to fast. Afterwards, there are special Id parties, with new clothes, gifts, and delicious food.

Id-ul-Adha

The festival of Id-ul-Adha takes place at the end of the yearly Hajj pilgrimage (see page 19). It is celebrated by Muslims all over the world.

A selection of Id-ul-Fitr greeting cards.

In some Muslim countries, a Bismillah ceremony is held when a child is about four years old. This is a very special day when the child learns to read the Qur'an for the first time. In front of family and friends, the child recites the first verse of the Qur'an and writes the alphabet in Arabic.

At this time, Muslims remember the story of Ibrahim ﷺ, told in the Qur'an. Ibrahim ﷺ was willing to sacrifice his son to show his love for Allah. Just in time, he heard a voice telling him to spare his son and kill a sheep instead. Today, a sheep or goat is killed, and the meat is shared among friends, family, and the poor.

Study and Reading

Reading and respecting the Qur'an

The word "Qur'an" means "reading" or "reciting." Muslims believe that it is their duty to read or recite the Qur'an in order to learn more about Allah and to receive His blessing. The Qur'an can be read or recited at almost any time and in any place. But it is vital to read or recite the Qur'an with one's whole body, heart, and mind, and to recite it carefully and clearly. The Qur'an is treated with great respect because it contains the word of Allah. When a copy is not being used, it is covered with a cloth and placed on a high shelf. No other books should be put on top of it.

Clean and pure

Before touching or beginning to read the Qur'an, Muslims must wash their faces, hands, arms, and feet, and wipe their hair with their damp hands. This is called wudu. It is taught in the Qur'an and in the Sunnah. Washing is believed to take away sins and to make worshippers clean and pure.

Rules for reading

Muslims can read the Qur'an in any comfortable position. Some readers sit cross-legged on the floor, with the Qur'an resting on a wooden stand in front of them. This shows respect for the Qur'an, which must never be placed on the floor. Many Muslims start their

Muslims wash before they touch or begin to read the Qur'an, and before they enter the mosque.

"So when the Qur'an is recited, then listen to it and pay attention that you may receive mercy. And remember your Lord within yourself in humility and in fear without being apparent in speech—in the mornings and the evenings. And do not be among the heedless." (SURAH 7: 204-205)

reading with a verse asking Allah to protect them from Shaytan. Then they recite the Bismillah. If the Qur'an is recited out loud to a group, the listeners must be silent. Even if they do not understand every word, they may be moved and inspired by the verses.

Mosque school

Many mosques have a school attached to them where Muslim children study the Qur'an. Sometimes the teacher is the imam, who leads the prayers in the mosque. Children learn the Arabic language so that they can recite verses of the Qur'an by heart. They also learn the five daily prayers and how to perform wudu.

Old or worn-out copies of the Qur'an must never be thrown away. They must be disposed of carefully, showing respect. Old copies are never thrown into a garbage can, for example. They may be wrapped in cloths and buried, or shredded and burned. Some are stored in a safe place, such as the roof of a mosque. Copies are sometimes thrown into a deep river.

A Muslim boy learns to read the Qur'an.

27

glossary

Adhan The call to prayer which is made from the mosque. It is made five times a day, by a man called a mu'adhin.

Allah The Islamic name for God, in the Arabic language.

Angel A being created by Allah out of light. In Islam, angels are the messengers of Allah.

Arabic The language in which the Qur'an, the Muslim holy book, is written. All Muslims say their prayers in Arabic and recite verses in Arabic from the Qur'an.

Ayah A verse of the Qur'an. Ayat is the plural.

Bismillah The words "In the name of Allah, the compassionate, the merciful," which begin every chapter of the Qur'an, except the ninth.

Calligraphy A beautiful type of writing which Muslims use to decorate the Qur'an and other objects because they are not allowed to use pictures of human beings.

Fard Things or actions that are compulsory for Muslims, such as praying five times a day.

Fasting Going without food or drink.

Five Pillars The five duties performed by Muslims which sum up the basic teachings of Islam.

Hafiz Someone who has learned the whole of the Qur'an by heart. Huffaz is the plural.

Hajj The yearly pilgrimage to Makkah that all Muslims try to complete at least once in their lives.

Halal Anything that is allowed or permitted, according to Islamic law.

Haram Anything that is not allowed or not permitted, according to Islamic law.

Hijrah The migration, or departure, of the Prophet Muhammad ﷺ from Makkah to Madinah in 622 C.E. It marks the beginning of the Muslim calendar.

Id-ul-Adha The festival of sacrifice that is marked at the end of the Hajj.

Id-ul-Fitr The festival that celebrates the breaking of the fast at the end of Ramadan.

Imam A Muslim who leads prayers in the mosque and gives a talk at midday prayers on Friday.

Jibril The angel who brought the words of the Qur'an to Muhammad ﷺ. Also known as Gabriel.

Jinn A being created by Allah out of fire. Jinns can be good or bad spirits.

Ka'bah The cube-shaped building in the Grand Mosque in Makkah. Muslims turn to face it whenever they pray.

Khadijah The Prophet Muhammad's ﷺ first wife.

Laylat-ul-Qadr The Night of Power on which the Prophet Muhammad ﷺ received the first revelation of the Qur'an.

Madinah A city in Saudi Arabia. Next to Makkah, it is the second holiest city in Islam.

Makkah The city in which the Prophet Muhammad ﷺ was born, and the holiest city in Islam.

Mosque A building in which Muslims meet and worship. In Arabic, a mosque is called a masjid.

Night Journey The amazing journey made by the Prophet Muhammad ﷺ from Makkah to Jerusalem.

Pilgrimage A journey made to a holy place by the followers of a religion.

Prophet A person chosen by Allah to teach people about Allah's wishes for the world.

Ramadan The Muslim month of fasting.

Revelation An experience in which an important teaching or truth is revealed, or made clear.

Salah Praying five times a day, at times specified by Allah in the Qur'an.

Sawm Fasting from just before dawn to sunset during the month of Ramadan.

Shahadah A sentence that sums up what Muslims believe. It is often called the declaration of faith.

Shari'ah Islamic law which is based on the Qur'an and the Sunnah.

Shaytan Another name for the Devil.

Sunnah The life, customs, thoughts, and actions of the Prophet Muhammad ﷺ. Muslims try to follow his example.

Surah A chapter of the Qur'an. In total, there are 114 surahs.

Ummah The worldwide community of Muslims.

Wudu The Muslim practice of washing before touching or reading the Qur'an, or entering a mosque.

Zakah An annual donation of money which must be made to a worthy cause by all Muslims who can afford it.

Index